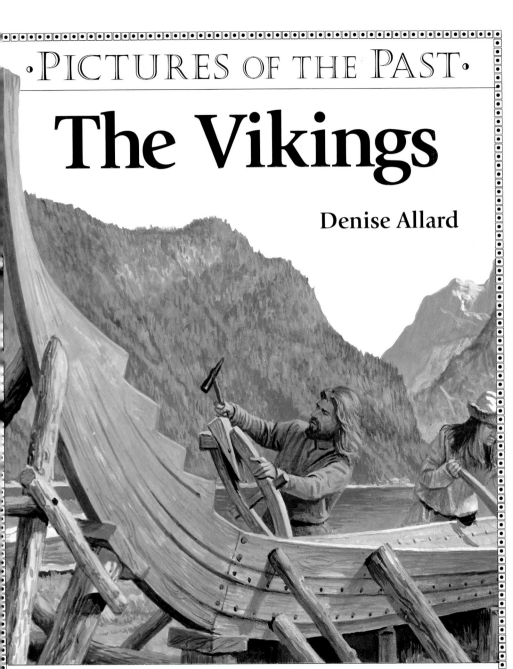

· PICTURES OF THE PAST ·

The Vikings

Denise Allard

Gareth Stevens Publishing
MILWAUKEE

For a free color catalog describing Gareth Stevens Publishing's list of high-quality books and multimedia programs, call 1-800-542-2595 (USA) or 1-800-461-9120 (Canada). Gareth Stevens Publishing's Fax: (414) 225-0377. See our catalog, too, on the World Wide Web: http://gsinc.com

Library of Congress Cataloging-in-Publication Data

Allard, Denise, 1952-
    The Vikings / Denise Allard.
       p. cm. — (Pictures of the past)
    Includes index.
    ISBN 0-8368-1717-6 (lib. bdg.)
    1. Vikings—Juvenile literature. I. Title. II. Series:
Pictures of the past (Milwaukee, Wis.)
DL65.A57   1997
948'.022—dc21   96-46231

This edition first published in 1997 by
Gareth Stevens Publishing
1555 North RiverCenter Drive, Suite 201
Milwaukee, Wisconsin 53212 USA

Original © 1995 Zoë Books Limited, 15 Worthy Lane, Winchester, Hampshire, SO23 7AB, England. Additional end matter © 1997 by Gareth Stevens, Inc.

Illustrations: Roger Payne, Shane Marsh, and Clive Spong

Printed in the United States of America

1 2 3 4 5 6 7 8 9 01 00 99 98 97

Contents

Homelands

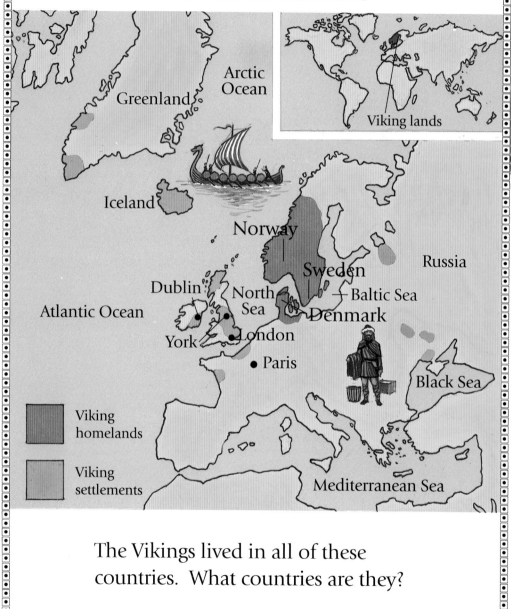

Arctic Ocean

Greenland

Viking lands

Iceland

Norway

Russia

Sweden

Dublin

North Sea

Baltic Sea

Atlantic Ocean

Denmark

York

London

Paris

Black Sea

Viking homelands

Viking settlements

Mediterranean Sea

The Vikings lived in all of these
countries. What countries are they?

4

Homelands

The countries of Denmark,
Sweden, and Norway have
seas around them. The
weather is often cold and wet.
Long ago, these countries were
the homelands of the Vikings.

The Viking people lived by
farming and fishing. They
built their homes near the
sea, and they visited each
other by boat.

Travel

How do people travel when they
visit other countries today?

Travel

The seas were very important to the Vikings. They caught fish to eat, and they sailed to many countries. Vikings were very good shipbuilders.

Researchers have learned about the Vikings from the objects the Vikings left behind.

At home

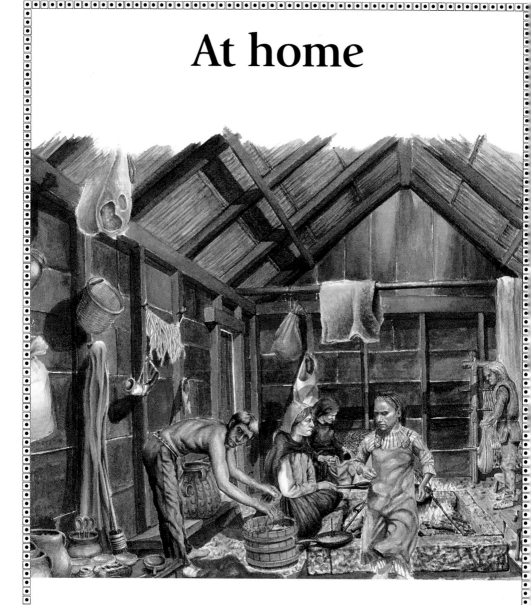

Vikings had to obey rules. Think of
some rules you have to obey.

At home

Viking families were often very large. Aunts, uncles, and grandparents lived together with parents and children. They all ate and slept in one big room.

The rules of a Viking village were decided upon at a meeting called a *thing*.

Daily life

What do you think the women
made from the cloth they wove?

Daily life

Most Viking people worked as farmers. The women did all the housework. They also wove cloth. Everyone worked on the farm, even the children.

Viking children did not go to school. They loved to sit beside a big fire and listen to grown-ups tell stories.

Farming

Everyone had to help on the farm.
What are these people doing?

Farming

Farmers grew vegetables.
They raised pigs, sheep, and
cattle. In autumn, farmers
stored food for people to eat
during the long, cold winter.

Viking farmers made tools
to use on their farms. Many
of the tools were similar to
those used today.

Food

The Vikings used these tools in the
kitchen. Name some of the tools.

Food

Because the Vikings lived near the sea, they often ate fish. The men fished all through the year. They also caught walruses, seabirds, whales, and seals to eat.

The Vikings ate vegetables, fruits, seafood, and other meats. They also ate cheese, bread, and porridge and drank milk.

Selling

The Vikings sometimes traded goods
instead of using money.

Selling

In Viking times, some people earned a living by selling goods. They bought the goods, such as jewelry, in town. Then they sold the items to people on farms.

Small pieces of silver were used as money.

In towns

Vikings made many decorative objects,
as well as tools.

In towns

In towns, people often made goods to sell. They made weapons, tools, jewelry, and leather shoes. They also made wooden bowls, cups, spoons, and combs.

The Vikings loved to decorate these objects. They made swords with carved handles, and belt buckles covered with patterns.

Jewelry

Clothing was often decorated
with jewelry.

Jewelry

The Vikings loved to wear
jewelry. Everyone wore
brooches to fasten their
clothes. They wore rings,
bracelets, and necklaces.
Rich people wore lots of gold.

People wore plenty of clothes
to keep warm. Men wore
wool trousers. Women wore
long wool dresses.

Shipbuilding

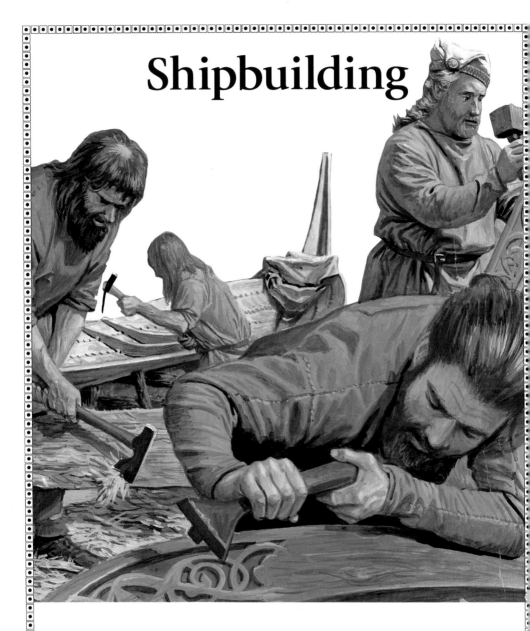

Viking ships were made of wood.
Decorations were added to the wood.

Shipbuilding

The Vikings built ships to carry goods to other countries. They also built fast warships and strong fishing boats. Shipbuilding usually took place during winter.

The Vikings used hardwood from oak trees to build their ships. Sails and oars moved the ships along.

Raiders

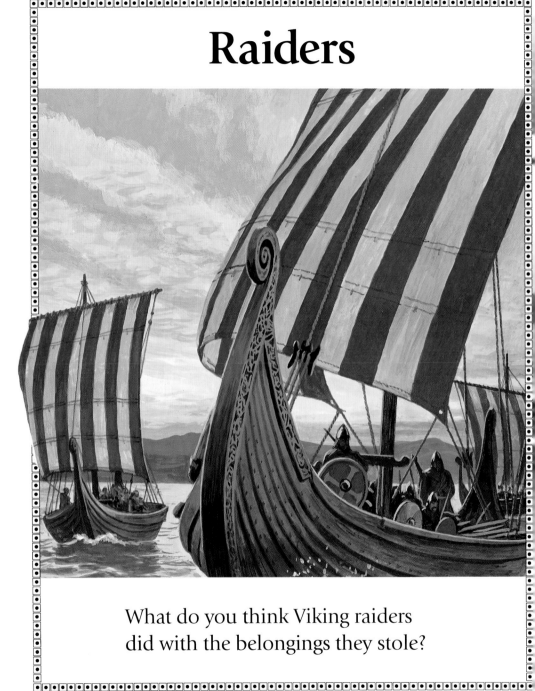

What do you think Viking raiders
did with the belongings they stole?

Raiders

Some Vikings crossed the sea and raided other lands. They stole animals, belongings, and even people. Everyone was afraid of Viking raiders.

The Vikings attacked with swords, battleaxes, spears, and large knives. They wore metal helmets.

Traders

Have any of the goods in your home
come from another country?

Traders

Many Vikings crossed the sea to buy and sell goods in other lands. They were called traders. They traveled as far as Russia to buy spices, furs, and silks.

Some of the goods Viking traders brought back from other lands have been found in Viking homes.

New lives

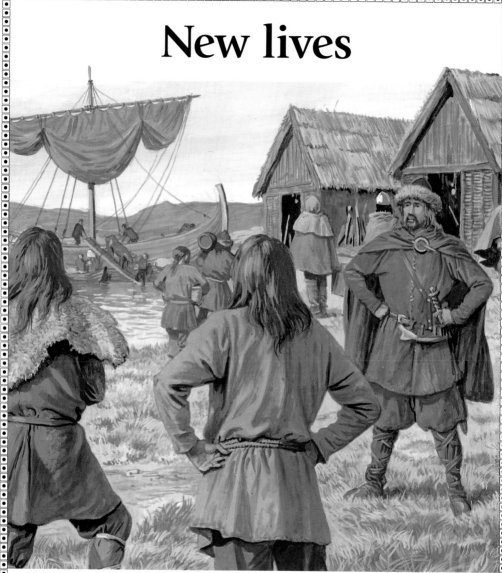

Vikings moved their families and all
their belongings by boat.

New lives

Some Viking families took their animals and moved across the sea. They went to live in other countries. There they built new homes and started new farms.

A Viking family lived in a house built from wood or stone. The roof was often made of straw.

Gods and goddesses

Vikings believed in many gods and goddesses.

Balder: the god of young people, beauty, and
goodness. He was the son of Odin.

Frey: the god of love and marriage. He was also
the god of sunshine and rain, and twin of Freya.

Freya: the goddess of love and beauty. She was
the twin sister of Frey.

Frigga: the queen of all gods and goddesses.
Frigga was the goddess of the sky and the
fireside. Her husband was the god Odin.
The word *Friday* comes from *Frigga's Day*.

Niord: the god of sailors and the ruler of the
wind. Frey and Freya were his children.

Odin: the wise chief of the Viking gods and
goddesses. He was the god of war and of poetry.
Odin was sometimes called Wodan. The word
Wednesday comes from *Wodansday*.

Thor: the god of thunder. He had a special
hammer that he used in battle. The Vikings
loved to tell stories about Thor. The word
Thursday comes from *Thorsday*.

Books

Everyday Life in Viking Times. Hazel M. Martell (Watts)

Leif Erikssohn and the Vikings. Charnan Simon (Childrens Press)

A Viking Settler. Giovanni Caselli (Peter Bedrick)

Viking Ships. John Lindow (Bellerophon Books)

Who Were the Vikings? Phil R. Cox (Usborne)

Videos

Viking Invasion and Yesterday's Journey, Volume 2. (Acorn Media Publishing)

The Vikings: Life and Conquests. (Encyclopædia Britannica Educational Corp.)

Vikings and Normans. (Films for the Humanities and Sciences)

Web Sites

http://control.chalmers.se/vikings/

http://www.ed.gov/pubs/parents/History/Home.html

Index